HOW TO TEACH SUZUKI PIANO

SHINICHI SUZUKI

MT746.S95 1993
Suzuki, Shinichi, 1898-
How to teach Suzuki piano
Secaucus, N.J. : Suzuki
Method International :
Distributed by Warner Bros.
Publications, c1993.

Warner Bros. Publications Inc.
15800 N. W 48th Avenue
Miami, Florida 33014

ISBN 0-87487-583-8

HOW TO TEACH SUZUKI PIANO

SHINICHI SUZUKI

—— Introduction ——

I deeply appreciate your participation in our efforts to educate children to a high level through researching human ability and music education. I encourage you and thank you for your continuous cooperation.

I'm writing this small brochure as a rough report of my research. I hope it will be of some service in your teaching.

——— Ability Development ———

First, I would like to explain my beliefs about human ability. It seems that most of us teach without an understanding of how human ability develops.

As you may have read in my book, every child can be educated. It has been proven many times that children raised in Osaka will automatically speak Osaka dialect. This is closely related to music education. Without exception, every child who is raised hearing beautiful pronounciation or music will learn to speak with just that inflection. This means that everyone can develop superior sensitivity and a true understanding of music if they are raised amidst high quality music.

It's very important to understand this and to educate parents concerning the importance of their children's listening to the teaching records. This is a test of your teaching ability. There are many people who may say that they understand this but never actually do anything. However, if these parents really understand what I am saying, they will play the records for their children. Those children who have been brought up in such a fine manner unconsciously have ability and become musically sensitive.

Next, I would like to discuss practice. Ability is developed through repeated practice. This means that ability is developed in direct proportion to the amount of practice. Also, children should practice willingly. It is most important to motivate them. This motivation depends on the teacher's skill in motivating the parents and children during lessons. Also at home, parents should help children to practice willingly everyday by praising them. A combination of the teacher's and parents' efforts is necessary. Therefore, teachers must educate beginners and their parents about this important aspect of the method to help children practice willingly.

Lessons are taken once or twice a week and are very short. The other six days, children practice at home. Ability is developed by home practice. Please understand this point and ask parents how children's practice is doing at home. To motivate the children to practice even more, both the parents and teacher must praise the child "How hard and well you are practicing these days!". I think this point applies not only to piano study but to every type of education.

—— The Belief That Every Child Can Be Educated ——

We are apt to have prejudices like "this child is no good," or "this child has talent." We must start by eliminating these prejudices and maintaining steady confidence that every human child can be educated and that there is no inherent talent. Every Japanese child can easily speak their mother tongue. We must not forget the general rule that ability can be developed if appropriate steps are taken, whether the ability developed is for good or bad. If children are raised by a wolf, they will develop wolf-like behaviour and be like animals.

We find a similar situation in the relative ability of our right and left hands. Generally, the right hand has very delicate coordination which allows us to write and do many things. However, the left hand is more poorly developed because it hasn't been trained. This doesn't mean that our left hands have less ability by nature, but that the difference is a result of how the hands have been trained in our daily life.

Please remember that every child can develop ability depending on the way in which they are raised, and like our right hands, be brought up to be highly sensitive and humanitarian. This is the basis of my educational method.

—— The Development of Musical Sensitivity ——

During lessons, if you feel that a child's musical sensitivity has not been sufficiently developed, please point out that they don't listen to the records enough. Developing musical sensitivity is the basis of music education. Please remember that students with poor musical sensitivity reflect a weakness in your own teaching. I always pay special attention to this point. In music education, a child with no musical sensitivity is as difficult to imagine as an Osaka child who cannot speak Osaka dialect.

The most effective and suitable way to develop sensitivity is to have children listen every day to recordings of high quality performances. This is really a very simple and easy method of education. Children absorb repeated stimulation from their daily life, just as they master their mother tongue. One's mother tongue is mastered not by knowledge or thinking, but directly through one's senses. Thirty-seven or thirty-eight years of experience have convinced me of this. I have attempted to obtain piano training records which are performances of the highest musical quality. Therefore, I am always searching for recordings of beautiful performances by artists of high musical sensitivity to include as instructional material for our students. I hope that in the future, great pianists all over the world will record performances for the Suzuki Method teaching materials.

—— The Importance of Tonalization ——

For vocal musicians, "vocalization" or training to improve the quality of the voice is a very important part of the lessons. After completing this training, vocalists study how to sing. Because I thought that a similar method should be used in teaching instruments, I asked the head teachers of the American String Teachers' Association (ASTA) to coin "tonalization" as a new English word.

The purpose of tonalization is to develop a beautiful singing tone, with a resonant *forte* and *piano*. First the teacher teaches children how to play the melody with a beautiful tone, using only the right hand. Next, children are taught how to play with the left hand. In this way, children develop the habit of listening to their own sound as they play.

In traditional musical training, students play while looking at a musical score. Such music has poor tone quality and no spirit, as if it were produced by a typewriter. Some students seem to think that making music means simply playing all the notes without mistake. To avoid this situation., we must teach students how to produce a beautifully modulated tone through tonalization training.

As with the violin books, fine piano works have been collected together to form the Suzuki Method Piano Books. Children get a great deal of pleasure from playing beautiful music. Therefore, considering technical factors, we carefully selected works of high artistry and musical quality which will appeal to children. Some teachers in the Piano Research Group have requested that etudes be added to the piano repertoire, however I think the repertoire itself is sufficient. This is because etudes have not been used in the Suzuki method to supplement the violin books for at least twenty years. Although studying etudes can be of some value, etudes have both a positive and negative influence on music education. For teaching the violin, I have created a system in which I arranged great works on the basis of their technical aspects. While recognizing the worth of practicing etudes, we must not forget the importance of music as music. I am thoroughly convinced of this.

My method is based on "mother tongue education," and of course there are no etudes by which babies learn to say "mama." Of course, the correct combination of words into sentences involves technical grammatical factors. However, as a child's vocabulary grows, they master grammar naturally. Careful consideration of this process of mastering one's native language can teach us very important things.

During the eight years that I was in Germany, I practiced for five hours a day, spending three hours each day on etudes. Why didn't I practice real music for all five hours? I deeply regret that I wasted countless hours in technical rather than musical efforts, when the music that I practiced every day contained technical factors equivalent to the etudes. Please understand that it is unnecessary to study Beyer and Czerny because the Suzuki Method piano repertoire was constructed taking into account the necessary technical factors.

In my violin teaching, when an advanced student has some technical weaknesses, I sometimes recommend that they study a few specific etudes. By the time a student becomes able to play concertos, there is enough technical practice contained within the concertos themselves. Therefore it is much more effective and economical to study the piece itself and learn to play it splendidly.

In teaching piano, I think that children's motivation suffers from the negative effect of practicing uninteresting etudes. This is an important point to consider.

In conventional music teaching, often this piece and then that piece is assigned to the student without adequate forethought concerning appropriate sequencing. The Suzuki Method Books have been carefully structured in an appropriate technical sequence which also attempts to develop superior musical sensitivity and performing ability. Therefore, it is important to study these books thoroughly and well. Let's continue to investigate better and more effective teaching methods. Please do not take the attitude that one only needs to learn how others are teaching to improve one's own teaching methods. I ask that each of us continue to actively study and research this area and share our ideas as members of a group effort to improve our methods of teaching.

—— Important Teaching Points ——

The important teaching points of the Suzuki Method may be explained as follows:

1. Teach in such a way that from the beginning children study each piece until they can play it very well. This teaching method develops children's ability.

2. Develop in the student a sensitive and accurate feeling for rhythm and tempo. This evolves through frequent listening to the teaching records, and the teacher's own rhythmical example.

3. Teach the student how to play with fine musical expression and a singing tone, how to make each note resonate, and how to produce a difference in tone volume between *forte* and *piano*.

When a child learns to play each piece well, it means that their ability to play is being developed. When a child has learned to play a new piece through by memory, I say "Well, now you've finished preparing to study this piece. Now let's study it in earnest. Listen very carefully to the record and study the rhythm and tempo so that you can play it beautifully next week." Then next week I say "You can now play the rhythm quite well, but please listen to the expressiveness of the tone shading on the record, and next week try to play it a little better than the record." This is the way in which I teach. Sometimes it takes quite a long time before the student is able to play the piece really well. However, when the student finally masters the piece, this ability has truly become a part of them.

From the point of view of developing ability, the worst possible thing a teacher can do is assign the next piece when a student has mastered only the notes of the previous piece and still plays it poorly, unmusically, and disinterestedly. Such teachers believe that moving from one piece to another in true progress, but it is impossible to develop ability in this way. I think that it is very poor teaching to leave earlier pieces without learning to play them excellently. One of the major weaknesses of previous methods of piano teaching has been that the importance of rhythm and tempo, and the overall quality of a student's performance has been forgotten in favor of rapid advancement from piece to piece. Please understand this very important point.

In the beginning stages, the speed and level to which a student polishes a piece must be in accordance with their ability. As they advance, their musicality, sense of tempo, and expressiveness will develop, and they will progress gradually faster and faster. A student's ability can be developed infinitely, in proportion to the ability of the teacher.

Please carefully consider these three teaching points which I consider to be of the greatest importance.

—— The Importance of Motivation ——

As in teaching any subject, motivating the student is very important, and I consider it the first and most crucial issue. Especially in the case of small children who may begin to take lessons before their own desire to learn has been aroused, the teacher and mother should together make every effort to have the child look forward to and enjoy the lesson. Please do not approach teaching in a severe and cold manner, but consider both the lesson and home practice sessions as a form of enjoyment for the child. At first, preschoolers have a short attention span, and it is best to stop at once when the child's attention wanders. If at this point the parents or teacher try to push the child to continue playing, the child will gradually begin to dislike lessons. Please stop the lesson within the child's attention span, praising him or her "You played very well." Such praise is very important in encouraging motivation, and therefore even if child does not play very well, it is best to find something about their effort that you can praise. Please remember "Don't push, don't scold, and don't forget to praise."

There are many techniques and ideas for motivating students. Watching other children's lessons while waiting for one's own is very effective. Children pick up many things from what they hear and see, and are inspired by watching the older students. I often ask an older student to play the piece that the younger child is studying. This is a very effective way to motivate students.

Another method we use is to have a "Day of the Week Concert." For example, every two months, all the children that have their lesson on a particular day of the week (such as Monday) give a small concert in the studio instead of having their regular lesson. The audience is made up of the other students and their parents. Each child plays a piece that he or she plays particularly well. If such concerts are set for every two months, the teacher can ask students at their lesson "Would you like to play this piece at the next concert?" In this manner even students who don't practice very much will practice hard for the concert.

This means that rather than teaching piano in the traditional private one-on-one manner, we must devise ways to help children study enjoyably in the company of their friends. When several children who play particularly well manifest themselves, they motivate the other students and raise the atmosphere of the entire group. If a group of such students appears, it makes the teacher's job much easier.

Instead of the traditional method in which children perform in a concert only once or twice each year, this "Day of the Week Concert" greatly encourages children's motivation and affects their attitude toward daily practice. Won't you try it?

—— The Use of Musical Scores ——

Because I often receive questions about teaching children to read music, I would like to explain my thinking and approach on this subject. The ability to read music is one important aspect of musical ability. However, the printed score must never be confused with music itself; it is nothing but a symbol of it. I believe that true music reading means discovering the composer's musical idea and expressing it aloud in a beautiful manner. For example, everyone recognizes a speaker of the Osaka dialect because they use a special lilt, nuance, and accent characteristic of that region. When a person from Tokyo reads a transcribed version of Osaka dialect, this is not the same as real Osaka dialect because it lacks that special lilt.

Nobody teaches a baby to talk by starting with printed letters and words. The natural order is to teach letters and reading after a child learns to talk. In the same manner, in teaching piano to preschool children, we do not use printed music, but rather have them learn new songs from listening to the record and showing them how to use their fingers. Mothers should be taught to read music however, because they need this skill to help their children practice.

Because music is something that we appreciate aurally, it is important to teach it as an aural medium. When using one's eyes, the ears are less attentive. If you play the piano in the dark, you become more aware of different musical inflections and nuances. The habit of practicing while reading music lowers students aural sensitivity and they tend not to listen to their own playing, in the manner of a typist.

Please teach mothers to read music so that thay can help their child learn new pieces, but wait to teach the student until an appropriate age and time. Until that time, I think that it's more important to develop the ear so that children listen to and judge their own sound, use an expressive *forte* and *piano*, and have a fine sense of tempo and rhythm. The goal of instruction is to develop students who depend upon the sound of a piece rather than upon a musical score.

Later, after we have taught children to play notes from looking at a musical score, we must teach them the habit that once they have learned a piece from a score, they should continue to study and perform the piece from memory. In my own teaching, I only assist students with that part of the piece which they can play from memory. If one uses this method until it becomes a habit for the students, it develops their memory and gives them the ability to play without a musical score.

In my teaching experience, some very diligent and highly developed students have been able to learn and memorize in one week long and difficult works such as the first movement of the Sibelius Violin Concerto, the entire Tchaikovsky Concerto, or the first movement of the Brahms Violin Concerto. Most advanced students are able to do this.

This type of ability is much less likely to be developed in a student who always relys on a musical score. It is very important to remember the goal of developing in students the ability to quickly memorize and play pieces with confidence once they have learned them from a musical score. I do not believe that reading music is unimportant, but as in the relationship between letters and sentences, I believe that it is also necessary to develop the abilities which underlie reading music.

This means that the teacher should first explain musical notation to the mother and teach her how to read the score. The child should listen often to the record, and if there are difficult passages, the mother gives assistance.

In this way, the child will come to play musically, listening to his or her own sound and musical expression. If such powers of discrimination are developed, when children do use a musical score, they will be able to do so to produce real music.

It is also probably necessary to practice sight reading. However, this comes after .the child's basic ability has been developed, as mentioned above. If students have fine musical understanding and sensitivity, they will be able to catch the real music from the musical score, which is after all the true meaning of reading music.

TEACHING THE BEGINNING STEPS

This chapter summarizes the major points about teaching the Suzuki Method discussed by teachers in the Piano Research Group during training courses at various places in Japan.

Please incorporate these points into your lessons considering the points Dr. Suzuki makes in the first section of this brochure.

1. Start from how to bow

In every endeavor, it is important to get off to a good start. Both children and their parents are nervous at their first lesson and don't know what they should do. It is important to help them relax while setting up a habit of correct lesson behavior from the very beginning. First, we teach the children how to bow. Students stand facing the teacher, say "Please teach me, Mr. (or Ms.) ——, " and execute a proper bow. When bowing, the child bends the upper part of the body at the waist in a slight angle. Until the child can bow correctly, do not proceed. This is an essential part of every Talent Education lesson, and is an important part of the curriculum in itself. We also ask that children bow to their mothers at home each day before they practice. As they practice each day, little by little their bowing improves.

At the end of each lesson, students again stand facing the teacher, say "Thank you very much," and bow again. This training helps to nurture good manners and a proper attitude and teaches proper lesson behavior. Experienced teachers say that whether or not a child bows properly is reflected in their attitude and ability to learn the lesson material.

After a child can bow properly, we teach how to sit in the chair at the piano with proper posture, and how to place the hands on the keys. When teaching small children, two or three years old, this must be repeated again and again. Sometimes entire lessons consist of only bowing, sitting and placing the hands on the keys. The goal is to teach proper lesson behavior and attitudes. Loving firmness on this point will help children learn how the teacher expects them to behave during lessons. This is a very important and necessary part of beginning lessons.

2. Make much of the basic "Twinkle Twinkle"

Proper instruction on the first piece is very important. Teach it slowly and thoroughly, without hurrying to finish it. First, teach taka-taka-ta-ta using only the index finger of the right hand. Practice until each tone is heard clearly, teaching the student to feel the bottom of the key. If a child's tone is small or indistinct, ask them to make a more solid tone saying "I can't hear you." It is very important for the teacher and mother to help the child learn to make a good tone from the beginning. Please do not teach a shallow tone to your students.

After ensuring that each tone is true and clear and the rhythm solid, we may proceed to teach taka-taka-ta-ta with the left hand in the same manner as with the right. If the first step is carefully and thoroughly completed, each succeeding one becomes easier. Even after the children progress to more advanced levels, they should study the Twinkle Variations each day as tonalization practice to improve their tone. If a teacher follows these teaching principles, both student and teacher will make effective and enjoyable progress during lessons.

3. Teach only as long as the child can concentrate

When teaching very small children, the teacher should take the attitude that learning the piano is enjoyable. Also, because preschoolers' attention span is likely to be very short, do not push them to continue the lesson beyond their ability to concentrate fully. You should end the lesson when you see their attention begin to wander. In this manner, we gradually lengthen the child's attention span.

4. Continue to study review pieces

This is an important aspect of the Suzuki Method. Students continue to study and review pieces they can play comfortably, to make them more musical and precise. Such careful building of one piece upon the other is the only method of practice by which students' abilities can be developed to a high level. Children should progress to the next piece only after the teacher sees that their ability is improving in this manner. The goal of the Suzuki Method is not to make children progress quickly through the repertoire, but to solidly develop true ability.

In fact, such continued study of review pieces helps children to progress more rapidly, and ensures that they can play beautifully any piece that they have already studied. It also improves their concentration and memory, and makes them more confident in themselves.

Of course, as the number of pieces the child has studied continues to increase, it becomes impossible to constantly review every piece. When the child reaches this stage, teach them to continue to study the previous two or three pieces without fail. Of course, this is in addition to continuous careful study of Twinkle and tonalization.

5. Correct weak points using easy pieces

When a teacher wants to correct some aspect of a student's playing, use a previously learned piece which the child can play comfortably. This makes it possible to correct such problems as hand position or tone production smoothly and without encountering resistance. If the teacher uses a new piece to demonstrate such points, the student becomes confused, and the teaching is ineffective. If there are a number of weak points to be corrected, choose the most central one and remedy it first. When that point is completely corrected, point out the next one.

6. Have children listen to the teaching records every day

Another special characteristic of the Suzuki Method is the importance of having students listen to the teaching records every day. This is something new in the history of music education, but it is a simple and very effective method of developing superior musical sensitivity.

Through listening to recordings, children learn both the pieces they are currently studying, and those they are preparing to study. Teaching is much easier and children progress much faster if they already know the melody, rhythm, and harmony of a piece before they begin to study it. One of the reasons that Suzuki Method students play so musically and with such obvious enjoyment is that they listen to the records every day. Similarly, in violin classes, a large gap develops between those who listen to the records every day and those who don't. For this reason, all Talent Education teachers agree on the crucial importance of listening to the practice records every day.

In teaching a piece which is not part of the recorded teaching material, the teacher should find a high-quality recording of the piece for the student to study. If this is not available, the teacher should record their own performance for the student. It is very important to urge the student to listen to the teaching records daily. To this end, request mothers to play the records before home practice sessions. The more children listen, the more effectively they learn.

7. Restudy from the beginning

Even an advanced student who has studied piano in the traditional manner should begin again from the beginning if they start taking lessons in the Suzuki Method. They need to learn the basic fundamentals of the Suzuki technique, and also how to play without a musical score. Even through they may have advanced to the level of Bayer in the traditional manner, they should study each piece, beginning with Twinkle. Because they already know something about how to play, they will be able to advance rather quickly and soon catch up with the other students.

8. Cultivate a group of exemplary students

Some teachers say that they would first like to test the Suzuki Method using one of their own children, or just one or two experimental students. In fact, however, it is very difficult to teach in this way. Instead, I think it is much better to gather a group of 5 or 10 people and begin to teach them all together. In the process of teaching, the teacher will gradually gain experience and become more confident. Some students pay close attention to the teacher's instructions and study very hard, and some don't. Also, because the level of the mother's understanding and cooperation directly affects the child's progress, some children progress more quickly than others. However, every child who learns through the Suzuki Method will rapidly develop ability. Gradually, through the process of teaching, the teacher will understand how to relate to the children and their mothers.

When a teacher finds that she has a number of particularly hard-working students who play very well, these students will raise the level and atmosphere of the teacher's entire group of students by providing a good example. Through observation, the younger students will gradually learn the nature of study and progress more rapidly. Please encourage the presence of such exemplary students if at all possible.

9. The importance of mothers' cooperation

Lessons are taught once a week, or in the case of very small children perhaps twice a week. This means that each week actual teaching occurs for only 5 minutes to 20 or 30 minutes at the longest, and the student must study at home the other six days of the week. If a child listens to the record and practices one hour each day, the total study time is seven hours per week. Because it is only through listening to the records and practicing that a child's ability develops, we can understand the importance of home practice. It is crucial that mothers understand this point.

To make the most of home practice, mothers whose children take Suzuki Method piano lessons make a tape recording of their child's lesson to remember the teacher's instructions. This tape is then used to refer to during home practice sessions.

10. Piano technique

There are no inflexible rules concerning the technical aspects of the Suzuki Piano Method. However, it is important that teachers clearly understand the nature of the Suzuki Method itself. Dr. Suzuki often tells his students "Your real teacher is Kreisler and I am only his assistant." He has his students listen to Kreisler's records and helps them learn how to approach his tone and expression.

Dr. Suzuki's highest goal is that students should become better than their teacher. A teacher's task is to nurture his or her students to a high level, both musically and as human beings.

11. Graduation System

The graduation system is unique to the Talent Education Institute. It is very important both from the teacher's point of view and in motivating students to study. It consists of the following levels and pieces:

Beginning Elementary Course

    Bach   Minuet No. 2

Elementary Course

    Clementi   Sonatina Op. 36-3

Pre-intermediate Course

    Bach   Two Minuets and Gigue
                    (From Partita No. 1 in B Flat)

Intermediate Course

    Mozart   Sonata in A Major K. 331

Advanced Course

    Bach   Italian Concerto

Master Course-First Level

    Mozart   Concerto in D Major (Coronation)

Master Course-Second Level

    Bach   Partita No. 1 in B Flat

Master Course-Third Level

    Beethoven   Sonata No. 33 (Appassionata)

Each piece should be performed in its entirety.